Women
WHO BELIEVE

Cover image *Guiding Light* by Annie Henrie Nader. For more information, go to AnnieHenrie.com.

Cover design by Christina Marcano © 2022 by Covenant Communications, Inc.

Published by Covenant Communications, Inc.
American Fork, Utah

Copyright © 2022 by Heather B. Moore and Angela Eschler
All rights reserved. No part of this book may be reproduced in any format or in any medium without the written permission of the publisher, Covenant Communications, Inc., P.O. Box 416, American Fork, UT 84003. This work is not an official publication of The Church of Jesus Christ of Latter-day Saints. The views expressed within this work are the sole responsibility of the author and do not necessarily reflect the position of The Church of Jesus Christ of Latter-day Saints, Covenant Communications, Inc., or any other entity.

Printed in the United States of America
First Printing: March 2022

28 29 26 25 24 23 22   10 9 8 7 6 5 4 3 2 1

ISBN 978-1-52442-174-8

Women Who Believe

Messages of Joy from the Sermon on the Mount

HEATHER B. MOORE *and* ANGELA ESCHLER

To the EE Team: You are more than colleagues and even more than friends. I am so grateful to have you as spiritual sisters and brothers with whom I joyfully walk the path back home.
—*Angela*

To the women in my life who have been an example of living the gospel with fortitude and faith: my grandmothers, mother, daughters, nieces, cousins, mother-in-law, sisters, sisters-in-law, and many dear friends.
—*Heather*

ACKNOWLEDGMENTS

The kernel of this project began a few years ago, and during the brainstorming and writing process, we had many discussions of what the Savior's teachings meant to both of us—as women—and how we personally applied them to our lives. This led us into the direction of wanting to write about the Sermon on the Mount and the way women could use the Savior's teachings to guide and strengthen them. With this in mind, we asked several women of all ages and walks of life to give us feedback on the manuscript. Special thanks to Michele Preisendorf, Gayle Brown, Lorie Humpherys, and Lisa Shepherd. Our publisher has been supportive of this project from the beginning, and we are deeply grateful for such a great team, including editor Ashley Gebert, cover designer Christina Marcano, managing editor Samantha Millburn, and the rest of the staff who work tirelessly to bring such inspirational books to readers.

INTRODUCTION

Come unto me, all ye that labour and are heavy laden, and I will give you rest. Take my yoke upon you, and learn of me . . . and ye shall find rest unto your souls.

For my yoke is easy, and my burden is light.

—Matthew 11:28–30

In the second year of Christ's ministry, after His baptism by John the Baptist, and following the forty days spent in the wilderness fasting while withstanding Satan's temptations, Christ spent His days and nights teaching, preaching, and curing all manner of sickness throughout Galilee.[1] With His healing physical, emotional, and mental ailments, it's no wonder Jesus Christ soon garnered a multitude of followers seeking comfort, healing, and wholeness.[2] These multitudes of men, women, and children were not only looking for physical healing; they were also seeking emotional healing from their trials and the spiritual strength needed to feel peace and joy on this earthly journey.

How can we obtain this same type of healing and peace? One way is to learn from those who have experienced similar trials who were able to endure and find joy using the principles of healing the Savior offered anciently and still offers today. In our own study of the subject, we focused on the women in the scriptures—specifically Ruth, Sarah, Abish, Hannah, Esther, Eve,

Sariah, and Mary—as examples to us today. In ancient times, these women dealt with weaknesses and trials on their mortal journeys, yet they found joy and gratitude in recognizing the paths to peace that Christ had laid for each of them. These paths include blessings that, at first glance, are difficult to recognize as such. But they are the key to peace now and in the eternities.

What are these blessings, and where can they be explored? Among the many teachings of Christ to the beseeching multitudes, it is interesting to note that He felt one set of principles to be so important that, in addition to revealing them in the Sermon on the Mount before His Crucifixion, He repeated them when He appeared on the American continent after His Resurrection;[3] they appear in the scriptural record both times, despite abridgments by ancient Nephite prophets. Why are these Beatitudes so important to us as to be preserved in these ancient records for modern times?

Because through the Beatitudes, Christ delivers a road map for how to become holy. Just like in the hymn "More Holiness Give Me,"[4] where we yearn for more patience, more faith, more joy, more gratitude, more trust, and more meekness, the Beatitudes offer the blueprint, so to speak, of what that journey to holiness looks like. And to what end do we desire the journey? As with our Elder Brother, holiness gives us new eyes to see. And that fresh, eternal perspective on our struggles means we can also develop new courage and a new heart filled with both peace and love.

We may not be at the physical location of one of Christ's greatest teaching moments, on the Mount of Beatitudes, but we can learn just

> *... holiness gives us new eyes to see. And that fresh, eternal perspective on our struggles means we can also develop new courage and a new heart filled with both peace and love.*

as much, have the same blessings bestowed upon our heads, and gain the peace and joy Christ promised through exploring the Sermon on the Mount.[5]

As we study the Beatitudes, we learn that each beatitude begins with the phrase "blessed are," which, translated from the Greek term *makarios*, means "happy" or "eternal joy." What if we focused on the translated version and instead of reading the Beatitudes as "blessed are," we read them as "happy are"?

> Happy are the poor in spirit: for theirs is the kingdom of heaven.
>
> Happy are they that mourn: for they shall be comforted.
>
> Happy are the merciful: for they shall obtain mercy.

With this singular adjustment, each of the Beatitudes takes on a deeper meaning. Each blessing, or covenant of happiness, suggests that we can find joy when the skies in our lives are murky—or black as night. As we will see in our discussion of the women of the scriptures, feelings of despair can be replaced with peace. As President Russell M. Nelson has taught us, "The joy we feel has little to do with the circumstances of our lives and everything to do with the focus of our lives."[6] If the focus of our lives is the Savior, then, indeed, the gospel of Jesus Christ is still *good news* because we are His, and He has already "overcome the world."[7]

Holiness cleared His mind and His path and allowed Him perfect communion with the Father. As we study both the Beatitudes taught by the Savior and the women who benefited from their principles, we find that the groundwork for obtaining peace and happiness in our lives has already been laid. The Beatitudes offer paths to happiness perhaps because they are also paths to *holiness*, and each is distinct in the lessons it teaches and the grace it leads us to find.

With this focus, even the bleakest days of our lives may, as the Prophet Joseph was promised during his own dark night, "give [us] experience, and shall be for [our] good."[8]

Despite the many sorrows and trials of the women in the scriptures and in our modern lives today, we can take solace in the fact that this road has

He comprehendeth all things, and all things are before him, and all things are round about him; and he is above all things, and in all things, and is through all things, and is round about all things; and all things are by him, and of him, even God, forever and ever.
—D&C 88:41

been paved before us. Christ has "descended below all things"[9] and suffered "temptations of every kind."[10] He both sympathizes and empathizes with us because He has walked the proverbial mile in our shoes. But even more comforting, "He comprehendeth all things."[11] This means the Savior knows the way through and the way out.

By studying the Beatitudes, we get a glimpse through the lens of holiness that guided "Jesus the author and finisher of our faith" through all the pitfalls and pains of this world, "who for the joy that was set before him endured the cross."[12] If the Savior can descend below all and all that darkness can be turned to His good, can we not in our personal Gethsemanes have faith in the path of holiness He sets before us?

Therefore, joy and peace are something we can experience *while* living in difficult circumstances or dealing with hard challenges. The words of the Sermon on the Mount have been preserved for thousands of years to comfort and guide us. By studying the meaning and significance of the Beatitudes, our faith will grow. That faith will, in turn, give us more holiness, "more purity . . . more strength to o'ercome, more freedom from earth-stains, more longing for home. More fit for the kingdom, more used would [we] be, more blessed and holy—more, Savior, like thee."[13]

SARAH

Blessed are they that mourn: for they shall be comforted.

—Matthew 5:4

Empathy and sympathy for another's plight can go a long way in helping someone through days of trial and grief. The Savior demonstrates this over and over throughout His ministry as He cares for His brothers and sisters upon the earth. In bestowing blessings and granting miracles, the Savior brings comfort to those in mourning, assuring them there is a brighter future.

In the book of Genesis, we discover that Sarai, wife of Abram, is probably a hopeful bride who comes to depend on the Lord in her marriage.[14] Like most women in ancient Israel, Sarai values becoming a faithful wife and mother during her days upon the earth. But the years pass, and she remains barren.[15] Her body cannot bring forth the children the Lord has promised her husband; He has told Abram he will become a great nation[16] and that his seed will inherit his lands.[17]

The defeating years pass as Sarai remains barren and mourns over not being able to provide posterity according to the Lord's promises. When she is seventy, Sarai makes the difficult decision to give her husband her handmaid Hagar. The "law of Sarah"[18] indicates that the decision was hers alone, and "Abram hearkened to the voice of Sarai."[19] This meant his posterity would be continued and the Abrahamic Covenant fulfilled.

Not only does Sarai give Abram her handmaid Hagar in order to bear children in her name, but Sarai also endures watching another woman do what she cannot: bear a son. We can only imagine Sarai's feelings of being neglected by the Lord when Ishmael is born to Abram and Hagar. Still, Sarai waits, and still, she must wonder where her place is in her home and in her husband's heart.

When Sarai is ninety years old and Abram one hundred, the Lord changes their names to Abraham and Sarah, then promises Abraham that Sarah will conceive a son. In response, Abraham falls "upon his face, and laugh[s]"[20] at the improbability of conceiving a child at their advanced ages.

But Sarah does conceive, becoming a living manifestation of the Lord's promise. When she bears Isaac, she becomes witness to a true miracle. Yet even with this remarkable and miraculous event in her life, her hardships are not over. Troubles abound between Sarah and Hagar, with the handmaid claiming her son Ishmael has the birthright and continually "mocking" Sarah.[21] Hagar is cast out by Abraham, but even after that, Sarah's trials are far from over.

Years later, the Lord commands Abraham to take his son Isaac to the altar on Mount Horeb and there sacrifice him. Does Sarah's mourning and questioning of God's will reach new depths? Does she wonder if she'll ever see her husband and only son again? She must have asked if this would be the last time she'd embrace her son or hear him speak.

Again, in her days of waiting for news about her son, her comfort can come only from the Lord. Another sweet miracle graces her life on the day Abraham returns with their son, whole and alive.

In *Jesus the Christ*, we read that "the mourner shall be comforted for he shall see the divine purpose in his grief, and shall again associate with the beloved ones of whom he has been bereft."[22] Perhaps this was how Sarah was able to bid her son farewell on his way to Horeb. Who knows what personal revelation the Lord bestowed on her to help her understand, to help her cope, and to help her give her will over to the Lord. Like Sarah, we can also take comfort in knowing that this earthly life is not the end but continues beyond death.

Sarah, in becoming the mother of Isaac in her advanced years, verified that nothing is "too hard for the Lord."

—President Russell M. Nelson

Yet mourning makes us weary and is draining to our emotional and physical health. Slowly, our strength will be restored, but we need the Lord's help for it to be so, for He is the embodiment of strength and endurance. In the words of Isaiah, "Hast thou not known? hast thou not heard, that the everlasting God, the Lord, the Creator of the ends of the earth, fainteth not, neither is weary? there is no searching of his understanding. He giveth power to the faint; and to them that have no might he increaseth strength. . . . But they that wait upon the Lord shall renew their strength; they shall mount up with wings as eagles; they shall run, and not be weary; and they shall walk, and not faint."[23]

Our moments of trial and hardship will be recompensed through the divine plan set forth by a loving Heavenly Father. When we have been weighed down with grief, we might be on the receiving end of comfort and service. Other times, we act on behalf of the Savior and bring comfort to a family member or a dear neighbor or a friend.

How to become like the Savior is explained by the Savior Himself in the Sermon on the Mount. As we contemplate how He blesses those who mourn, it's important to take a step back and understand that mourning a loss or tragedy can be very lonely. Thus the Savior has promised that those who mourn will be comforted because He is the way to comfort, peace, and joy.

Still we might ask ourselves, "Why me?" or "How could this happen when I've been faithful?" Many times, we won't be able to answer these questions in this lifetime but must look to the broader perspective and closely consider the eternal nature of our beings in order to trust in the comfort offered by the Savior and by those who may come to our aid.

> *To Sarah . . . I say,*
> *"Thank you for your*
> *crucial role in fulfilling the*
> *purposes of eternity."*
> —Elder Jeffrey R. Holland

Sarah had the right to ask all these questions, and as she remained faithful even in her mourning, she became a witness to how the Lord always keeps His promises. In Sarah's twilight years, she could no doubt look back upon her life and see the blessings that had sprung from her days of mourning: the Lord had not forgotten her; she had been preserved to bring forth Isaac; and through her and Abraham's seed, all nations would be blessed.

As we reflect on Sarah's life of blessings and trials, we see that she was not alone in her mourning. She was never alone. God was mindful of her and kept His promises. Her husband was also there to mourn with her. When others mourn with us, we feel less alone, and through this shared empathy, we feel the love God has for us. In this way, we become the embodiment of Christ as He endured earthly suffering. We can see beyond the vicissitudes of this earthly life, as Sarah learned to do, and can feel at peace knowing we are moving forward in the plan of salvation, salvation that is available to all. Eventually, the deep grief eases into acceptance, then understanding, and finally peace in this life and greater peace in the next.

RUTH

Blessed are the meek: for they shall inherit the earth.

—Matthew 5:5

In the book of Ruth, we find a story of loss transformed into abundance—a story that echoes the beatitude of inheriting the earth through meekness.

The widow Naomi has lost her husband and both her married sons while away from their homeland. For women with no male provider in ancient times, this meant a desperate fight for survival with no right to land, employment, or other legal or financial protections.

Given that she may have merciful kinsmen and possibly greater support if she returns to her native home in Bethlehem, she sets out on the dangerous journey, notwithstanding her advanced years. Reading between the lines, we see that Naomi was a kind and compassionate mother-in-law to the daughters her sons married, even though these daughters were not of her faith or culture, and it was a time of great prejudice against those who were different: "Naomi said unto her two daughters in law, Go, return each to her mother's house: the Lord deal kindly with you, as ye have dealt with the dead, and with me. The Lord grant you that ye may find rest. . . . Then she kissed them; and they lifted up their voice, and wept."[24]

The women wept some more, and then Orpah kissed her mother-in-law and departed, likely pursuing support from her kin similar to what Naomi planned to seek in Bethlehem.

"But Ruth clave unto [Naomi]," saying, "Entreat me not to leave thee, or to return from following after thee: for whither thou goest, I will go; and where thou lodgest, I will lodge: thy people shall be my people, and thy God my God: Where thou diest, will I die, and there will I be buried: the Lord do so to me, and more also, if ought but death part thee and me."[25]

We must pause and wonder at the meekness and charity of this young woman to not only abandon all security she may have found in returning to her own parents' home and possibly remarrying among her kind, but also to honor and accept the beliefs and culture of another in the desire to serve and care for Naomi.

What gave her such strength? What quiet whisperings of the Spirit might she have experienced in hearing of Naomi's God? What promptings toward faith? And what courage it must have taken to still lean toward that fledgling faith after losing her husband and future in one dark moment. Both Naomi and Ruth were dealing with great fears and grief—having lost all. As Naomi told her neighbors upon returning home, "Call me not Naomi, call me Mara. . . . I went out full, and the Lord hath brought me home again empty"; *Naomi* means "pleasant," and *Mara* means "bitterness" or "very sad."[26] Despite these heavy burdens, Ruth meekly committed to care for another and face an uncertain path.

As the days in their new home passed, the uncertainty over their ability to survive would also have been very great. Yet the tale does not indicate that Ruth railed against an unjust God or lashed out in regret or resentment that she faced such a predicament on another's behalf. On the contrary, she seemed to accept what was and looked for opportunities to help more. When Naomi thought of a kinsmen who had barley fields, Ruth suggested, "Let me now go to the field, and glean ears of corn after him in whose sight I shall find grace."[27]

This was akin to begging, where the poor and widows would follow the barley harvest and glean the inferior bits of sheaves and stalks left behind by the reapers in an attempt to have something with which to make bread.[28] One wonders if it was difficult for Ruth to swallow her pride in order to do such a thing. We don't know her background with her own people—if she had been well regarded, respectable, possibly admired, etc. We don't know what social class she came from or what she sacrificed in worldly and psychological comforts to care for Naomi. While we cannot know how difficult it was for Ruth to humble herself to this degree, we can imagine it was not easy to publicly beg for food. But her spiritual strength is also evident, as humility goes deeper than just swallowing our pride.

Humility is not only to submit to God's will but to participate fully in building the kingdom of God on Earth—being willing to serve and be served. What does such meekness feel like? To be teachable, to not speak vainly or seek attention, to happily serve wherever called, to lift others, and to seek the will of God; there is a quiet peacefulness embedded in these descriptions. But it grows even more from there: it is an act of courage in our time when attitudes centered around "me first" and "why me?" are prevalent. As Elder Bednar states, "The Christlike quality of meekness often is misunderstood in our contemporary world. Meekness is strong, not weak; active, not passive; courageous, not timid; restrained, not excessive."[29]

> *A model of ideal womanhood is Ruth.*
> —President Thomas S. Monson

Perhaps in her many months of suffering, Ruth's meekness and willingness to trust in her new faith activated grace and made her burdens bearable, much like the people of Alma in the Book of Mormon: "And . . . the Lord did strengthen them that they could bear up their burdens with ease, and they did *submit cheerfully and with patience to all the will of the Lord.*"[30]

And then we reach a turning point in her narrative where the story transforms into one of hope. For, as Ruth is gathering sheaves of grain day after tiring day, Boaz, another kinsman of Naomi and one who oversees the fields, notices her. He instructs his servants to leave

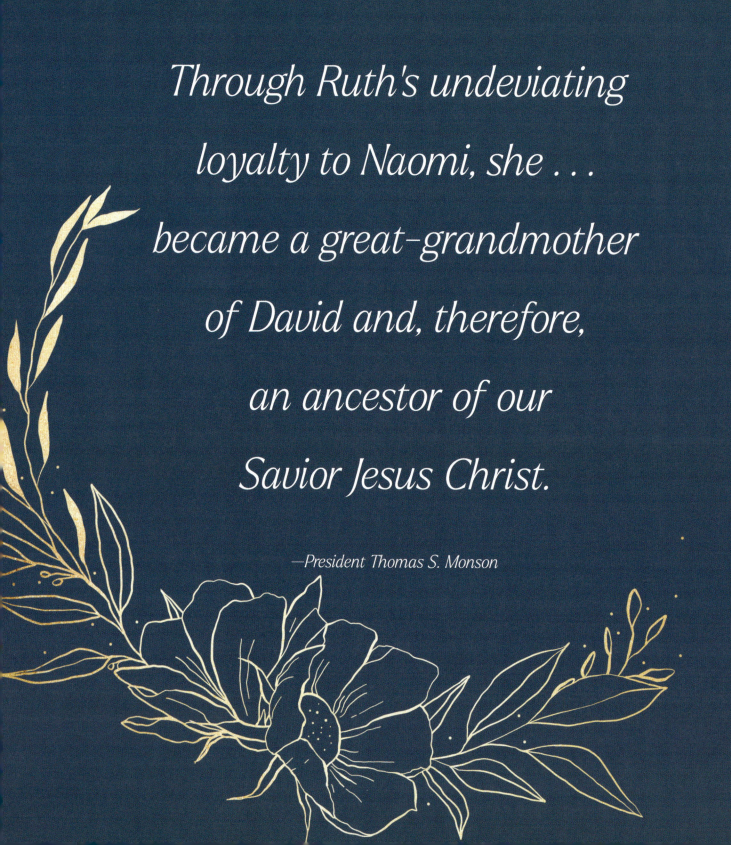

Through Ruth's undeviating loyalty to Naomi, she ... became a great-grandmother of David and, therefore, an ancestor of our Savior Jesus Christ.

—President Thomas S. Monson

her the better part of the grain as she gathers, and he gives her permission to rest and take food in the shade of his buildings. Her response? "Then she fell on her face, and bowed herself to the ground, and said unto him, Why have I found grace in thine eyes . . . ? And Boaz answered and said unto her, It hath fully been shewed me, all that thou hast done unto thy mother in law since the death of thine husband: . . . The Lord recompense thy work, and a full reward be given thee of the Lord God of Israel, under whose wings thou art come to trust."[31]

His kindness, similar to Ruth's own toward Naomi, evolves over the course of the following verses into one of deep respect and possibly love and affection. Naomi, sensing this, and with compassion for her daughter-in-law after all her unwearying care, says to Ruth, "My daughter, shall I not seek rest for thee, that it may be well with thee?"[32] And then she bids Ruth to participate in a ritual of asking for protection and aid through marriage.[33] The ending is a happy one, reversing Ruth's and Naomi's circumstances from physical and emotional poverty to temporal, emotional, and spiritual abundance. And the story closes with the birth of Ruth's son, who, by the traditions of the times, would ensure his female family members were cared for ever after—and who continued the royal lineage of the Caregiver of us all.

In our final review of Ruth's meekness, perhaps we can be instructed through greater familiarity with one of its signs; patience is part and parcel of meekness, which can help us turn our own suffering, through grace, into joy. As gospel scholar Wayne Brickey once put it, "The patience of faith is called long-suffering. Is it painful? No, quite the opposite. Because patience invites meaning, dignity, and the companionship of heaven, it relieves pain of mind. It enables us to last. . . . It bends meekly before the necessary and stands firm before the unnecessary, never cowering or pouting. It inherits the earth."[34]

EVE

Blessed are they which do hunger and thirst after righteousness: for they shall be filled.

—Matthew 5:6

"Now the serpent was more subtil than any beast of the field which the Lord God had made."[35] Not fully understanding God's plan and eager to bring suffering to mortals, Satan approaches Eve, asking why she hasn't eaten from the tree of knowledge of good and evil. When she replies that she and Adam will die if they eat of that tree, Satan counters, "Ye shall not surely die: For God doth know that in the day ye eat thereof, then your eyes shall be opened, and ye shall be as gods, knowing good and evil."[36]

And so the story of mortality begins; Eve eats the fruit and initiates the Fall. But was it that quick and simple? Eve's story is fascinating, partly because she is the first woman to face mortality and navigate all its slings and arrows, difficult decisions, and sorrows.

Since ancient times, misperceptions of Eve's wisdom and righteousness have reigned. But through later scripture and the restored gospel, we know much more about the righteousness that drove her agency in the garden. Eve's innate hunger and thirst for knowledge beautifully set the stage for the Savior's promise in the Sermon on the Mount: *Blessed are they which do hunger and thirst after righteousness: for they shall be filled.*

Surely Eve was "filled" in many ways through her mortal experiences, but the journey to ultimate fulfillment through peace and joy was, no doubt, rocky.

We need women who … express their beliefs with confidence and charity. We need women who have the courage and vision of our Mother Eve.

—President Russell M. Nelson

Mistranslated scripture and misguided culture claim Eve was deceived and had poor judgment. But Hebrew scholar Dr. Nehama Aschkenasy notes that the Hebrew word currently translated as "beguiled" in the King James Old Testament was originally a rare verb form no longer in use but indicating complex meaning. Dr. Aschkenasy summarizes that it is "safe to say [the word] indicates an intense multilevel experience which evokes great emotional, psychological, and/or spiritual trauma."[37] This was not a simple decision based on a wily trick of the adversary! This word makes it "clear that [Eve's choice after the serpent beguiled her] was motivated by a complex set of inner drives" that caused her to step back and reevaluate.[38]

While we have only translations of ancient text to rely on in guessing at the internal process Eve may have gone through, it does seem possible that the decision to partake of the fruit could have caused her to reevaluate and perhaps cope with inner distress; as we know, not only did the serpent's answer counter what she thought she knew, but she now faced two seemingly conflicting commandments—not to eat of the tree and yet to replenish the earth (which required she eat of the tree to become mortal).

Over time these conflicting instructions may have gained layers of meaning and complexity for her. Is it possible that the conversation with that great serpent took place weeks, months, or even years before she decided to partake of the fruit—that Adam and Eve's tutoring may have taken time (even centuries) before they were properly prepared to face one of the greatest decisions of our collective history? We will never know how long their tutoring took, but we do know they talked with the Lord with a degree of familiarity during their time in the garden and that He taught and commanded them during this era.[39]

Eventually Eve chose to follow the higher law. As Elder Boyd K. Packer taught, "the Fall came by transgression of a law, but there was no sin connected with it."[40] To elaborate, laws—whether of nature, the legal system, or as commandments from God—function on different levels in the context of human experience. Whereas the violation of some is *inherently* wrong, the violation of others may have consequences but may not be immoral in nature: you will suffer consequences when violating the law of gravity, but it is not immoral to fall.

As Moses 3:17 states, Adam and Eve were forbidden to eat of the fruit, lest death come, but then were told, "Nevertheless, thou mayest choose for thyself, for it is given unto thee." This particular wording clarifies that only agency would break the laws keeping them from becoming mortal; it could not be a simple accident or innocent failure to grasp the implications. Neither could godly force start our mortal journey that was to follow the great war that preserved our agency.

And so, "when the woman saw that the tree was good for food, and that it became pleasant to the eyes, and a tree to be desired to make her wise, she took of the fruit thereof, and did eat, and also gave it unto her husband with her, and he did eat."[41] Let's pause to understand the word *saw*, in which Eve sees the tree for what it is. Scripture does not seem to be implying she *noticed* it for the first time, but rather that she's seeing it in a new light—through spiritual or wiser eyes. Sometime around this illumination she must finally understand her divine duty.[42] And in this moment, it is clear Eve hungers and thirsts for righteousness, for she chooses to give up the Garden of Eden and partake of the fruit with Adam.

Once the fruit was eaten, "the eyes of them both were opened."[43] In that opening, their transgression was complete. *Transgression* comes from the Latin *trans*, meaning to

> *Angels are still sent to help us, even as they were sent to help Adam and Eve.*
>
> —Elder Jeffrey R. Holland

"[move] from one . . . state . . . to another" or "beyond" or "across," and *gress* means "to go."[44]

Eve's hunger and thirst after righteousness may have started as a search for wisdom and knowledge, but as she grew in that wisdom, she discovered insight into her purpose, realizing it was she who had to make that difficult but necessary choice and that she and Adam would be proxy for all of mankind in this first great act of agency. Evidence that her righteousness followed a thirst for wisdom comes in her courageous adherence to the laws of sacrifice and consecration—the highest laws of love—made on behalf of her spirit brothers and sisters who had long awaited the day of her awakening.

As the heavenly doors opened to the spirits waiting in the premortal existence, the gates of the garden shut behind Eve. Eve's mortal journey was undoubtedly difficult. The scriptures note that Adam lived nine hundred and thirty years,[45] so it is likely Eve lived a similar number of years. Imagine all the tribulations of mortality lasting for centuries—and being the first woman to navigate them all! No how-to books, no Internet answers, no therapists, and no other women to check your emotions and experiences against.

Given the scriptural record, it seems clear that the hunger and thirsting after spiritual knowledge that started her journey into mortality must have been a foundational character trait in navigating an untamed physical and spiritual wilderness, the death of some of her children, and seeing other children carve dark paths. As with all of us, seeking wisdom and the comfort of the Holy Ghost would have been the North Star guiding her through such an uncharted life.

The promise of the Savior that those who hunger and thirst after righteousness will be filled is expanded upon in the Book of Mormon reframing of the Beatitudes. The promise is that they will be "filled *with the Holy Ghost.*"[46] Both the simple connotations of *filled*—content, not empty, made new—and the promise that the Holy Ghost will fill in the broken places in our hearts are no small comfort.

Do we thusly hunger and thirst after the righteousness that leads to powerful decisions, great wisdom and faith, and the strength of the Spirit in our lives, as was demonstrated by Mother Eve? Do we often feast on scriptures and doctrine or embrace the gift of the Sabbath, preserving it for stillness, holy study, and openness to inspiration? Do we look to consecrate our efforts in the benefit of our spiritual family everywhere?

Additionally, by study and by faith, women of Christ will need to learn to recognize the half-truths of the adversary, not only seeking to discern the full truth for themselves but also to speak up amongst their sisters, revealing logical fallacies and rhetorical sophistry disguised as enlightenment and advancement,[47] or stripping down ideas that falsely justify the reverse—excuses for suppression, abuse, or exploitation. While we must do so with compassion and reflection, to hunger and thirst after righteousness does require us to *act* on the knowledge we receive.

In contemplating her own great sacrifice, Eve "was glad, saying: Were it not for our transgression we never should have had seed, and never should have known good and evil, and the joy of our redemption, and the eternal life which God giveth unto all the obedient."[48]

May we choose our own small sacrifices, wrestle with our own difficult decisions, and be filled with the Holy Ghost as we follow Eve's footsteps from the garden to eternity, hungering and thirsting for righteousness and being "fed in rich abundance"[49] by the Savior of us all.

ESTHER

Blessed are the merciful: for they shall obtain mercy.

—Matthew 5:7

The Savior brings attention to the attribute of mercy in the Sermon on the Mount when He says, "Blessed are the merciful: for they shall obtain mercy."[50] The book of Esther is full of examples of strength, sacrifice, tolerance, love, and mercy. The principle of mercy plays a key role in the events of Esther's life and the lives of her people. Mercy goes hand in hand with Esther's charity as she "suffereth long" and "seeketh not her own."[51] Interestingly enough, mercy also comes from an unexpected source—the king of Persia—who has taken Esther to wife, making her his queen.

This is no fairy-tale marriage because Esther is second wife to the king of Persia. She must tread carefully on ground paved by generations of cultural norms.

In the king's first marriage, his wife, Vashti, refused to obey his request to come to his banquet and show herself. This probably meant he asked her to come without her veil, something Vashti would have traditionally worn. The king's advisers told him to divorce her because if the queen refused to obey the king, it would set a precedent for all the women in the kingdom to not listen to their husbands.[52] Often a king has to make hard choices in order to follow his own rules. In this sense, there was no room for the king to be merciful toward his own wife if he wanted to remain a respected and revered leader in his kingdom.

So the king began his search for a new queen, and after a series of events, Esther was chosen.

We might think it would be wonderful to be royal and live in a palace with a lot of wealth, but Persia was a dangerous place. The Persians were involved in major battles, and the Jews themselves were living in exile in Persia after being driven out of Jerusalem years before. The king's father had offered them a place to live, a place of refuge, in Persia.

There was probably some animosity between the Jewish people and the Persians because the Jews were guests in their land, and sharing the land would have taken some getting used to.

Esther is advised by her cousin Mordecai to keep her religious beliefs a secret from the king. This puts her in a tough spot because not only is she going into a new marriage, she can't openly practice her religious beliefs. Esther must have wondered what she would teach her future children. If she couldn't worship, they couldn't worship. She also had to be afraid that if her husband found out, he would be angry that she'd kept the information from him.

Esther is an orphan and is living with her cousin Mordecai and his family when she's discovered. So, really, Mordecai is her only family link until she gets married. And then she has to step into a new life, completely different than her life steeped in Jewish culture, and try to learn what's expected of her as a queen and wife.

Early in Esther's marriage, a dilemma arises. The king's right-hand adviser, Haman, calls for the banishment and subsequent annihilation of the Jewish people.

Now Esther finds herself in the middle of a decision that could very well destroy her life if she acts or destroy the lives of her people if she does nothing. She needs to look within in order to determine how deep her well of mercy is. For, according to Persian custom, Esther can't officially approach the king with a request unless she is invited. To approach the king without invitation is to risk being put to death.

How does Esther make such a monumental decision?

> *Esther, through fasting, faith, and courage, had saved a nation.*
>
> *—President Thomas S. Monson*

Let's learn more about the characteristic Esther has cultivated: mercy. If mercy is defined as suffering long and not seeking our own, we can conclude that sacrifice is the teacher of mercy. We see this displayed in Esther's life. She has already sacrificed by keeping her religion a secret after being chosen to marry the king. She's lived months and possibly years unable to worship as she believes, and if she's already borne children, she has raised them in a religion foreign to her. She's learned to withhold judgment and to love unconditionally. Yes, her life is certainly full of more wealth and privilege now, but the trade-off is dear.

Like the Savior in Gethsemane praying for mercy upon all of our souls, Esther finds herself turning to her Maker as well and pleading for mercy for her people. Men and women today may find themselves in situations where they have to make serious decisions about whether they will be merciful toward others and themselves and, in turn, receive mercy from the One.

In this vein, Truman Madsen asks, "Will we resent or repent? Will we permit his mercy and his long-suffering to have full sway in our hearts and bring us down to the dust in humility?"[53] Since mercy is so closely tied to humility, this is why Esther must now turn inward and seek out the true wishes of her heart. If she wants mercy extended to her people, she must put her own well-being on the line and approach the king, just as we have to seek mercy from time to time and, in exchange, also give mercy to others. For strength, Esther turns to fasting and prayer. She has been patient and tolerant and now must act.

The time has arrived for Esther to reveal her true identity to her husband. If she doesn't, many people will either lose their homes or, worse, be killed. Since Esther herself is Jewish, she could technically be banished from Persia as well.

We see Esther's true character when she is faced with disaster in these verses: "Then Esther bade them return Mordecai this answer, Go, gather together all the Jews that are present in Shushan, and fast ye for me, and neither eat nor drink three days, night or day: I also and my maidens will fast likewise; and so will I go in unto the king, which is not according to the law: and if I perish, I perish."[54]

After fasting for three days and laying her burdens at the Lord's feet, she seeks out the king. In approaching him, she hopes he will allow her to talk to him. In Esther 5, we read,

> And it was so, when the king saw Esther the queen standing in the court, that she obtained favour in his sight: and the king held out to Esther the golden sceptre that was in his hand. So Esther drew near, and touched the top of the sceptre. Then said the king unto her, What wilt thou, queen Esther? and what is thy request? it shall be even given thee to the half of the kingdom. And Esther answered, If it seem good unto the king, let the king and Haman come this day unto the banquet that I have prepared for him.[55]

Esther's merciful attitude toward her people then lends itself to the king's mercifulness toward her and extends to all other Jews in Persia. The king listens to her plight and reverses the edict against the Jews in an action of mercy begetting mercy. This reinforces the principle that "mercy hath compassion on mercy and claimeth her own."[56] Esther's faith, determination, and willingness to sacrifice her well-being become a humbling illustration for us to learn from and emulate.

As President Dieter F. Uchtdorf counsels us, "Lay your burden at the Savior's feet. Let go of judgment. Allow Christ's Atonement to change and heal your heart. Love one another. Forgive one another. The merciful will obtain mercy."[57]

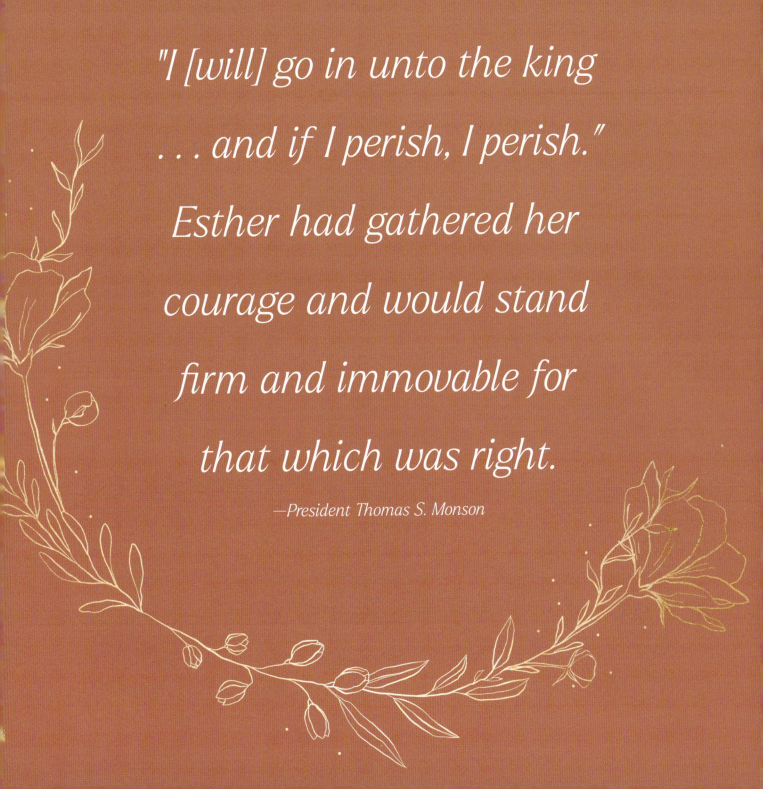

"I [will] go in unto the king . . . and if I perish, I perish." Esther had gathered her courage and would stand firm and immovable for that which was right.

—President Thomas S. Monson

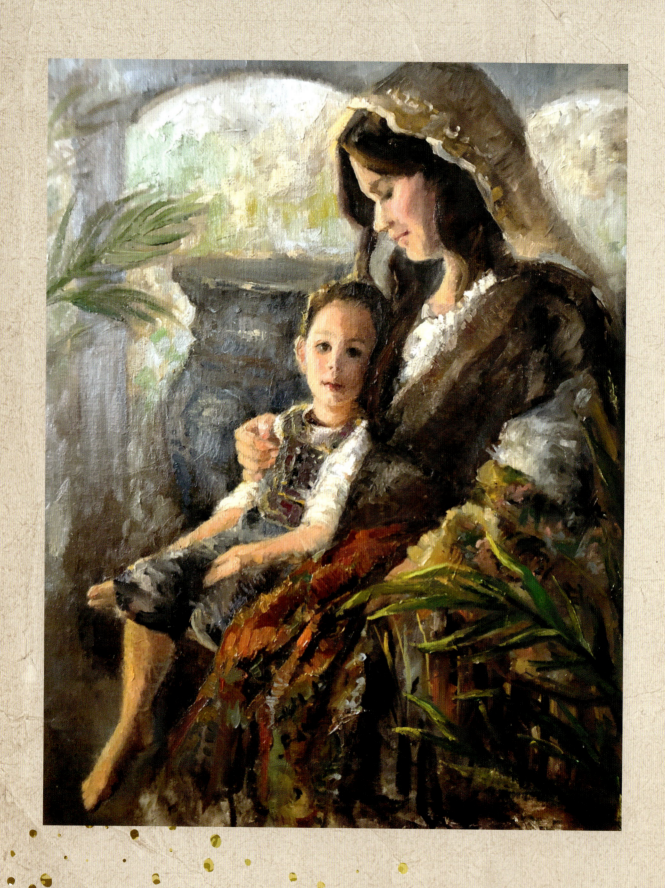

HANNAH

Blessed be the poor in spirit: for theirs is the kingdom of heaven.

—Matthew 5:3

Not all of us will face a time where there's not enough food on our table or when we are unable to pay the electric bill, but each of us will meet challenges that will humble us in such a way that we'll feel we are barely holding our heads above water. Because of this, we find deeper meaning in the beatitude "Blessed be ye poor: for yours is the kingdom of God."[58] We can be poor in spirit physically, mentally, and emotionally. President Harold B. Lee said, "The poor in spirit, of course, means those who are spiritually needy, who feel so impoverished spiritually that they reach out with great yearning for help."[59]

In the book of Samuel, we meet Hannah, the wife of Elkanah. Hannah has been barren for years, and without the knowledge of modern medicine, she likely believes she is cursed by God because she hasn't been blessed with children. Not only is she feeling spiritually impoverished, but in the biblical era, a wife's barrenness was grounds for divorce. To compound Hannah's distressing situation, because of her barrenness her husband marries a second wife, Peninnah, who vexes Hannah about her barrenness and "provoke[s] her sore,"[60] all while Peninnah enjoys the blessing of multiple sons and daughters.

It's no wonder Hannah takes on the mantle of becoming "poor in spirit." Hannah has much to grieve over, and her state of happiness becomes something nearly nonexistent, so much so that her husband is compelled to ask, "Hannah, why weepest thou? and why eatest thou not? and why is thy heart grieved? am I not better to thee than ten sons?"[61]

It's worth noting that her husband forgoes his right to divorce Hannah for her barrenness, which illustrates his genuine love for her. Even so, Hannah's grief is so deep she cannot eat. Not only is she mentally and emotionally struggling, but her physical health is also at risk.

In desperation, she pours her heart out in prayer and fasting, vowing that if she can but have a son, she will raise him as a Nazarite and consecrate his life to serving in the temple. In this way, Hannah is also vowing to turn her will over to the Lord and to redirect her life to all that is holy. Once she has made this tearful vow born of years of grief, the blessing she seeks arrives in the form of a temple priest.

Eli the priest spots the weeping Hannah while she is on her annual temple trip with her husband. At first Eli believes her to be drunk. When Hannah explains that she's not drunk but "a woman of a sorrowful spirit"[62] who is pouring out her soul in righteous prayer, Eli pronounces a blessing upon her. The blessing is simple and direct: "Go in peace: and the God of Israel grant thee thy petition that thou hast asked of him."[63]

Just as the Savior promises that the poor in spirit will be blessed and receive the kingdom of heaven, the transformation of Hannah's life becomes an example of this very blessing. The conception and birth of her son Samuel brings new feelings of gratitude in her life, which is now her very heaven on earth. In addition, she eventually has more children, another heavenly blessing. And through her "poor in spirit" pleadings, she receives the blessings of the kingdom of heaven in the form of eternal covenants kept. More importantly, she understands that God hears her and knows her hopes and desires. After the birth of Samuel, Hannah does not forget her promise to God to raise Samuel as a Nazarite, and she brings her son to the temple when he is of age.

Not all our pleadings to the Lord are answered in the direct and miraculous manner Hannah's was, but we can rest assured the Lord knows us on an individual basis and will bless us for our faithfulness. The Lord's timetable might be different than what we are hoping for, but like Hannah, we can place our burdens in His hands.

Many of us have pleaded to the Lord for specific blessings, just like Hannah and her desire for a "man child."[64] Many of us have experienced what it is to feel poor in spirit, where we are filled with humility, recognize our dependence on God, and bend our will to the Father's. Some of us might have short-term trials, while others face lifelong challenges.

What comfort can we draw from the Lord's promise of granting the poor in spirit the kingdom of heaven? We can realize that while our earthly challenges can be crushing at times, we have an eternal future to consider. By humbling ourselves and being willing to accept whatever the Lord will bless us with during our earthly sojourn, we can become like Hannah—full of gratitude. A witness to our Savior's love. Aware of our divine worth.

Let's remember that the fullness of the beatitude reads, "Blessed are the poor in spirit who come unto me."[65] Truman Madsen points out that "we are promised, you and I, that we can be among the noble and the virtuous and the pure in heart who will seek counsel and authority and blessing constantly from under His hand."[66] Like Hannah, who recognized she needed God's help, we, too, can seek counsel and blessings through fasting and humble prayer. She stripped herself of all pride, and only then was she open to completely accepting God's will.

If we can put away our pride and become poor in spirit, *our* hearts will be open to God's will.

The Lord's will may mean the fruition of our desired blessing, or it may mean an alternate path that strengthens us in an unforeseen way. We can take comfort in knowing that "they who keep their second estate shall have glory added upon their heads for ever and ever."[67]

In the same vein of this beatitude, we have been taught that "all things must come to pass in their time."[68] Whether our desired blessings are delayed

> *Samuel had a sainted mother, Hannah.*
>
> —Elder Cecil O. Samuelson Jr.

Just as Hannah . . . prayed fervently for her child, the value women place on motherhood in this life and the attributes of motherhood they attain here will rise with them in the Resurrection.

—Sister Julie B. Beck

for months, years, or even a lifetime, we will eventually receive our grand reward—a place in the kingdom of God as promised us by the Lord.

Times will arise when we feel poor in blessings, poor in opportunities, or poor in physical or mental health. In Luke 4:18, Jesus claims He is the one who is "anointed . . . to preach the gospel to the poor." We are all poor, are we not? We are all destitute in some form or another.

No matter which walk of life we hail from—poverty, wealth, or something in between—true happiness can be found in following the Savior. Our poor-in-spirit experiences will testify to that. Hannah was desperate for a blessing from the Lord, and wealth or privilege could not have fulfilled that desire for her, for the kingdom of God is priceless above all else.

MARY

Blessed are the pure in heart: for they shall see God.

—Matthew 5:8

> And in the sixth month the angel Gabriel was sent from God unto a city of Galilee, named Nazareth,
>
> To a virgin espoused to a man whose name was Joseph, of the house of David; and the virgin's name was Mary.
>
> And the angel came in unto her, and said, Hail, thou that art highly favoured, the Lord is with thee: blessed art thou among women.
>
> And when she saw him, she was troubled at his saying . . .
>
> And the angel said unto her, Fear not, Mary: for thou hast found favour with God.
>
> And, behold, thou shalt conceive in thy womb, and bring forth a son, and shalt call his name Jesus.[69]

What a mission to be presented with—to be told you are responsible for raising the Savior of the world! No doubt this was a heavy moment for Mary despite the awe and spiritual strength she may have felt.

As we know from later scripture, Mary is wont to ponder things, and from the angel's definition of her as "highly favoured," it's likely she was prompted toward purity of heart and seeking after God's will long before this calling ever came to her. Such purity of heart would have prepared her for the presence of angels and the Spirit. Additionally, while her simple answer to the angel belies the difficulty of what she was about to face, it also reveals her faith and familiarity with things of the Spirit: "And Mary said, Behold the handmaid of the Lord; be it unto me according to thy word."[70]

When we are likewise pure in heart, the Lord can use us to be His hands to fulfil the many missions we each have been given, whether they last a few months or a lifetime and whether they are a joy to fulfil or deeply difficult to manage. For Mary, her mission in life would have been all these things.

In the beginning, as she feels the miracle within her, and having likely been familiar with the scriptures and prophecies about the Messiah, her vision is expanded: "And Mary said, My soul doth magnify the Lord, and my spirit hath rejoiced in God my Saviour. For he hath regarded the low estate of his handmaiden. . . . He that is mighty hath done to me great things and holy is his name."[71]

But she would also likely have felt weighed down at times by her knowledge of what was to come. Indeed, the mother of the great Jehovah is forewarned of the heavy sorrows she will face. While her son is only a babe in arms, Mary takes him to the temple and receives this prophecy from a holy disciple of the Lord: "And Simeon blessed them, and said unto Mary his mother, Behold, this child is set for the fall and rising again of many in Israel; and for a sign which shall be spoken against; (Yea, a sword shall pierce through thy own soul also,) that the thoughts of many hearts may be revealed."[72]

How does Mary cope with the intense emotions that must have filled her heart, knowing the breadth and depth of her mission and that of her son's? One telling reveal is that with every great miracle and likely every heavy burden, Mary "kept all these things, and pondered them."[73] What was she pondering? Perhaps she contemplated the meaning of such miraculous moments for her sacred stewardship and of their significance for the family of mankind. Likely she also filled her heart with prayer.

Undoubtably part of Mary's purity before the Lord would have come from her turning to Him, perhaps for help, but also when repentance would

Mary ... "a precious and chosen vessel," ... knew more about [Jesus] than anyone else.

—Elder L. Whitney Clayton

have been required, as with all God's children. The "pure heart" is a phrase relevant to the process of purification and sanctification; as Truman Madsen noted, "no mortal can endure [divine] presence except quickened by the Spirit of God."[74] Thus, a pure heart is a consequence of a fundamental change in our desires and motives—not simply through increased self-discipline but through the grace of Christ after all we can do.

While pondering and prayer are important parts of purifying our hearts, the results of such may be even more significant. As Paul notes, we now "see through a glass, darkly,"[75] but as we become more like God, we will recognize the divine in others and see as God sees. And we will truly recognize the will and works of God as we strive to have a pure heart, because we can see God clearly only when we have a changed heart.

> *Mary, mother of our Redeemer, was the perfect example of complete submission to the will of God. She kept confidences. In faith, she endured grief.*
> —President Russell M. Nelson

What does it mean to have a pure heart? The scriptures suggest it is to be in a state where virtue garnishes our thoughts[76] and where we think no evil—seeing others with the love of Christ and viewing the world through a positive and hopeful lens.[77] Through the sanctifying power of the Holy Ghost, we will understand our weaknesses, know when it's necessary to repent, and open our hearts to the will of God. Through covenants and ordinances, we can work toward putting off the natural man, and through grace, we will obtain the "mind of Christ."[78]

As we grow into this state of Christlike vision, we will gain a new perspective of our difficulties and sorrows and be enabled to endure valiantly and steadily. Mary witnessed both great and terrible things in relation to her mission in life; no doubt her fear for her son's safety and the mortal consequences of His mission increased in tandem with her amazement at

His power and purpose. Watching her son grow to manhood and knowing His cup would be bitter and He would innocently suffer in both body and spirit would have torn at her motherly heart. But she had promised God in her youth: "Be it unto me according to thy word."[79] The result of that heart-wrenching yet glorious promise was that she would have come to understand God through her tragedies as she kept a believing heart. Her experience was as Job's, who said at the end of his trials, "I have heard of thee by the hearing of the ear: but now mine eye seeth thee."[80]

Facing our missions in life requires great courage, but the blessings that come from pondering the truth and striving for a pure heart will give us strength when we need it most. We may see God as He works miracles in our lives—not just in the obvious blessings we enjoy, but also in our own spiritual evolution and the development of our capacity to love and serve like He does. We may better see God as we recognize His miracles and tender mercies. And we may see God in the sense that our understanding of Him—from becoming more like Him—will help us to see a little more clearly through that dark glass of mortality.

It's difficult to comprehend the special way Mary saw God—how she may have understood the mission of the Savior and how hers intertwined with it. She saw God in all the spiritual ways we've noted, including through her deep trials, but she also quite literally saw the workings of God on Earth. In fact, as the only mortal witness of the Savior's entire life from birth to death, her words to her cousin Elizabeth have even greater meaning at the end of her life: "My soul doth magnify the Lord, And my spirit hath rejoiced in God my Saviour."[81] Indeed, with her pure heart, Mary would have seen her son and understood Him as the Son of God, for she would have looked "unto Jesus the author and finisher of our faith; who for the joy that was set before him endured the cross."[82]

We can endure our many trials, see and appreciate our many blessings, and hold before us that great, eternal joy as we come to count ourselves among the pure in heart—those *who shall see God*.

ABISH

Blessed are the peacemakers: for they shall be called the children of God.

—Matthew 5:9

The narrative of Abish in the book of Alma is a story of secret conversion and worship. Abish lives in the city of Ishmael—a Lamanite province ruled by King Lamoni. As a servant to the king's wife, Abish is privy to court life. This also means she's adept at knowing when to speak her mind and when not to, when to be a vocal peacemaker and when to keep quiet.

In the Sermon on the Mount, the Savior explains, "Blessed are the peacemakers: for they shall be called the children of God."[83] Abish is a testament to this promise when she becomes a peacemaker at a pivotal time in her people's history. In Abish's case, peace in the Lamanite royal court is a serious concern since some of the people are suspicious of Ammon—a Nephite interloper who has been teaching the plan of salvation among them, resulting in the king lying as if dead for three days.

Although King Lamoni has allowed a Nephite to enter his court and work as one of his servants, not all Lamanites agree with this allowance. Traditionally the Lamanites and Nephites are not friends, and if a former Nephite prince is somehow responsible for King Lamoni's death, war is inevitable.

Yet Abish is not able to share her knowledge of God with her people or provide the sweet relief of peace during these tense three days. Some of us may find ourselves in this type of situation—either we aren't able to openly live our beliefs in our communities or countries, or we're in family situations where our prayers and worship are done quietly. We then become peacemakers, or stewards, over our own hearts with a quiet assurance from the Lord that we're following a path of righteousness even when our environments are turbulent or our loved ones dwell in the "large and spacious building."[84]

There may be times in our lives when we diligently prepare, and even though we may not know exactly what our future might bring, we can be assured that being faithful will bless us exponentially. As we follow in the footsteps of the Savior, the Prince of Peace, and strive to be like Him, we will be blessed in the most eternal way: being counted among and called the children of God.

When Abish's father shared his "remarkable vision" with her, she became "converted unto the Lord."[85] Yet due to the political climate of the city of Ishmael, where the Lamanites have had to worship according to the king's beliefs, Abish would have been ostracized by her community and neighbors had she declared her testimony. Surely the introspection she must have gone through prepared her for a time when she could use her testimony in the role of a peacemaker.

Abish reaches a crossroads in her faith as she watches the events of Ammon's teachings unfold. After defending the king's flocks and slaying the king's enemies, Ammon is thought to be the Great Spirit.[86] At the king's behest, Ammon shares the plan of salvation in order to explain where his power truly comes from.[87] When King Lamoni falls to the earth as if dead, Abish does not dare speak up yet.[88] She is the queen's servant, and the queen is the one who must pronounce the king dead or alive.

The Lamanite woman Abish believed the "remarkable vision of her father."

—Elder Neil L. Andersen

In addition, if Abish speaks prematurely, her own people could very well turn on her. So she remains quiet for the time being. Ammon then declares that the king still lives, and on the third day, the king rises.[89] A changed man, King Lamoni shares his testimony, and then the queen is overcome by the Spirit.[90]

Now, Abish is on her own.

But her faith runs deep, and she is touched by the Spirit, as verse 17 demonstrates: "When she saw that all the servants of Lamoni had fallen to the earth, and also her mistress, the queen, and the king, and Ammon lay prostrate upon the earth, she knew that it was the power of God." The key word here is *knew*—Abish is *already* prepared. She already lived in the role of a peacemaker by living that peace within her own heart by keeping her testimony quiet until the time was right to share it. She knows *how* to recognize the Spirit's whisperings, and she understands that *now is the time*.

At last she can share her true beliefs, although she probably could never have predicted it would be done in such a public and urgent manner. After she runs from house to house to declare that the king and queen and their servants are not dead but are instead overcome by the Spirit of God, she returns to the royal palace to discover that a crowd has gathered.[91] Fear and accusations pulse through this crowd, and as during any uncertain time, rumors abound: a Nephite has conceivably caused the death of their Lamanite king and queen. In this way, "the contention began to be exceedingly sharp among them."[92]

The stress of what Abish must do reduces her "even unto tears,"[93] but she pushes forward despite her anguish. She reaches the unconscious queen and takes her hand, and at this single touch, the queen awakens and rises to her feet.[94] What a glorious, crowning moment in Abish's life. And it all began with something as small as a seed of truth and personal prayer in quiet corners.

No one can doubt that, at this moment, Abish was fulfilling her calling as a child of God.

President Russell M. Nelson said,

> Jesus declared that a day of judgment would come. All individuals will give an account of their mortal lives and of how they have treated other people" [See Matthew 12:36]. . . .
>
> . . . As a Church, we must "renounce war and proclaim peace." As individuals, we should "follow after the things which make for peace." We should be personal peacemakers. We should live peacefully—as couples, families, and neighbors.[95]

What does being a peacemaker look like in our lives? Does it mean looking for ways to collaborate? Listening to another person's viewpoint with an open heart and mind? Does it mean educating ourselves and striving to have charity toward our fellow men or women or families?

We see Abish's courage, prompted by the Spirit, to be a peacemaker. Not only is she a peacemaker among her employers but also among her people and country. If she hadn't stepped in, those in the crowd panicking with fear of the unknown could have easily rioted or declared war, leading to an entirely different outcome. Abish's accomplishment heralds in the message of the following verse: "Therefore, renounce war and proclaim peace, and seek diligently to turn the hearts of the children to their fathers, and the hearts of the fathers to the children."[96]

We are all children of God—this is a given. But it is a privilege to be *called* the children of God. This meaning is one step deeper, one step more personal, one step closer to God. As peacemakers, we will be sitting on the right hand of God, and "the right hand of the Lord is exalted."[97]

The power of Abish's conversion and testimony was instrumental in changing an entire society. The people who heard her testify . . . "were converted unto the Lord."

—Sister Elaine S. Dalton

SARIAH

Blessed are they which are persecuted for righteousness' sake: for theirs is the kingdom of heaven.

—Matthew 5:10

History holds a sacred and terrible record of those who have endured persecution for the sake of Christ and the gospel. From the ancient Saints in the Colosseum to the early Saints of the Restoration and today, we all fear the mob mentality. Perhaps some of us have already endured or will one day endure modern scenarios of persecution: public reviling, shaming, or the maligning of our character or the intentions of our hearts. Or, more dire, perhaps we have faced a physical threat to our or our family's safety due to our beliefs and values.

As terrible as those things may be, there is yet another form of persecution we may face in Christ's name: the painful and poignantly personal experience of prolonged rejection, mockery, or angry chastisement from those who should be most understanding of why we stand for righteousness—our parents, children, spouses, siblings, friends, and others we may deeply love. Often the personal attacks we face are added upon by the sorrow of seeing these dear ones lose their way and their once-soft hearts. When the gospel could heal them and our relationship with them, the outright rejection of such balm is a heavy weight on our souls.

Sariah, wife of the prophet Lehi and mother to Nephi, Sam, Laman, Lemuel, Jacob, Joseph, and at least two daughters, faces many of these forms

We will change the world. For the better. For this journey to great heights is not any ordinary journey, any more than was Sariah's.

—Sister Elaine L. Jack

of persecution after, and possibly before, she flees Jerusalem with her family. Under threat, her family must leave quickly and without their treasured belongings or even basic comforts. Imagine boldly sacrificing everything for your belief in Christ only to face years in a harsh, unforgiving wilderness and an uncertain future.[98]

Undoubtedly this was not a simple thing for Sariah to accept. A mother has many pressures and responsibilities. What of her children's safety? What of their futures? Would God really support them? It's likely that as the matriarch of the family, she prayed mightily in search of answers and comfort.

As she reckons with these questions and fears, there is also the subtle yet continuous pressure of family conflict; this trial of faith is breaking her family apart. Is that what God intended?

After all, how could she simultaneously show her sons her love while seemingly taking the side of her husband (with his visions), who had brought them into such a bleak situation? Were there days when she felt she had to choose between God and her family?

It is under these heavy circumstances that we see the pressures of an overburdened heart. The scriptures record a moment of deepest fear when she thinks her sons are dead and that, perhaps, God has abandoned them. Likely in tears and desperation, she questions Lehi's visions and conviction that they have done the right thing.

How many days passed as she wrestled with this question before the Lord brought her sons safely home? We feel empathetic relief for this obedient sister as she, possibly falling upon her knees, thanks her Father in Heaven, being comforted and coming back to herself: "And she spake, saying: Now I know of a surety that the Lord hath commanded my husband to flee into the wilderness; yea, and I also know of a surety that the Lord hath protected my sons."[99]

Yet there are still many long years ahead and heavy tribulations for Sariah to endure in the wilderness. Not only that, but once she reaches the promised land, she has to choose between two sets of families. The loss of one's children and grandchildren to hatred and rebellion would be enough to break any heart. Was Sariah eventually forced to extract herself from the troubled lives and conflicts of her loved ones when her son Nephi was commanded to flee from Laman and Lemuel? If she did leave with Nephi, was it—unthinkably—to protect herself from her own posterity? In addition to the pain such a choice would cause, did she then struggle with resentment toward those who had wounded her heart so deeply? What would any of us have done in her position?

One cannot endlessly put out emotional fires. It is likely she had to come to terms with the conflict and seek comfort in a more eternal perspective. This trial of her faith may have taught her much: to be not easily provoked; to forgive; and to be patient, calm, gentle, and respectful—to be a peacemaker.

If she was able to find her own peace in such circumstances, she likely did so by staying close to the Spirit. Truly Lehi was inspired in knowing their family would need the comfort of the scriptures in the years to come, and perhaps they were such a comfort for his widow.

As Sariah likely learned, our developing testimonies can turn into firm convictions as we seek holiness through any trial. President Henry B. Eyring has taught, "Greater holiness will not come simply by asking for it. It will come by doing"—and, we would add, *enduring*—"what is needed for God to change us."[100] And Elder Ulisses Soares affirms that even regarding "something you feel is undeserved, to take up one's cross and follow the Savior means to strive to lay aside these feelings and turn to the Lord so He can free us from this state of mind and help us to find peace."[101]

Of course, surrendering to the refiner's fire can be difficult; we don't ask for suffering, and we don't want to see our loved ones in pain or lost on dark paths, but the edges of even the greatest sorrows can, over time, be softened as we gain new eyes to see the wisdom and blessings that have come from each experience.

To have the Spirit soften the painful polishing of our lives is the only way to find rest in the Lord.

What does it mean to "enter into the rest of the Lord"? President Joseph F. Smith once spoke on the subject: "It means that through the love of God I have been won over to Him, so that I can feel at rest in Christ, that I may no more be disturbed by every wind of doctrine, by the cunning and craftiness of men . . . and that I am established in the knowledge and testimony of Jesus Christ, so that no power can turn me aside from the straight and narrow path that leads back into the presence of God." For that man or woman, your "heart is fixed; [your] mind is made up; doubts have been dispelled; fears have all been removed; [you know] in whom to trust."[102]

> *Like Sariah, we keep moving towards exaltation, the ultimate promised land.*
> —Sister Elaine L. Jack

As with Sariah, even amidst the greatest and ongoing persecution, we have the opportunity to enter into the rest of the Lord well before we pass through the veil. Despite ongoing years of struggle, she states unequivocally at one point what she has learned of the Lord: "Now I know of a surety."[103] She has an eternal perspective and knows in whom she can trust.

Brigham Young once spoke on the eternal perspective we will all one day have: "We talk about our trials and troubles here in this life; but suppose that you could see yourselves thousands and millions of years after you . . . have obtained eternal salvation. . . . [t]hen look back upon your lives here, and see the losses, crosses, and disappointments, the sorrows . . . ; you would be constrained to exclaim, 'but what of all that? Those things were but for a moment, and we are now here.'"[104] Does having an eternal perspective mean that we will cease feeling grief, anger, or fear, or will never struggle with a difficult decision, never plead for discernment over a complex, high-stakes issue? Likely not for most of us, but those emotions will have *reduced power over us*. How? The scales of mortal vision will fall from our eyes as we learn to fully trust in the Lord, become transformed through our trials, and truly recognize that "happy are" those who follow the path of holiness laid out in the Savior's Sermon on the Mount.

THE BEATITUDES

—Matthew 5:3-10

Blessed are the poor in spirit:
for theirs is the kingdom of heaven.

Blessed are they that mourn:
for they shall be comforted.

Blessed are the meek:
for they shall inherit the earth.

Blessed are they which do hunger and thirst after righteousness:
for they shall be filled.

Blessed are the merciful:
for they shall obtain mercy.

Blessed are the pure in heart:
for they shall see God.

Blessed are the peacemakers:
for they shall be called the children of God.

Blessed are they which are persecuted for righteousness' sake:
for theirs is the kingdom of heaven.

QUESTIONS TO PONDER

SARAH

Blessed are they that mourn: for they shall be comforted.

1. When Sarah, wife of Abraham, bid her son farewell on his way to Horeb, she didn't know if she'd ever see Isaac alive again. Somehow she had the strength and the faith to follow the Lord's will no matter what the result would be for her son, Isaac. Like Sarah, how can we take comfort in knowing that this earthly life is not the end but continues beyond death?
2. Sometimes we are the one enduring a hardship, and sometimes it's a family member, neighbor, or friend. What are some ways we can act on the Savior's behalf and bring comfort to others?
3. Through studying the Sermon on the Mount, we learn how to become like the Savior. What things stood out to you about how Sarah lived her life that is comparable to the Savior's life?
4. What do you think the Savior would say if you sat across from Him right now and asked why you've been given specific trials?
5. Just as Sarah was never forgotten by the Lord in her trials and mourning, neither are we. Which scriptures or counsel in this chapter can comfort us when we feel alone in our trials or mourning?

RUTH

Blessed are the meek: for they shall inherit the earth.

1. In the book of Ruth, we find a story of loss transformed into one of abundance—a story that echoes the beatitude's promise that we'll inherit the earth through meekness. In what ways did Ruth's meekness lead to inheritances both temporal and spiritual?
2. Ruth meekly committed to leaving all she knew, all that was safe and comfortable, to care for another in need. What do you suppose gave her such strength? How did she have confidence that something so unknown was the next right step for her?

Have you experienced answers to prayers, unexpected strength, or direction that enabled you to do what might seem terrifying or impossible through temporal eyes? Do you know of others who have experienced this?

3. Meekness is a complex trait, closely aligned with humility and patience. What does meekness look like? What traits or emotions come to mind? What fruit does it bear in our lives?

4. As Elder Bednar states, "The Christlike quality of meekness often is misunderstood in our contemporary world. Meekness is strong, not weak; active, not passive; courageous, not timid; restrained, not excessive."[105] In what situations might meekness be an act of courage or strength?

5. Meekness often means accepting the will and timing of God with patience and faith. Wayne Brickey noted that such "patience invites meaning, dignity, and the companionship of heaven, it relieves pain of mind. It enables us to last. . . . It bends meekly before the necessary and stands firm before the unnecessary, never cowering or pouting. It inherits the earth."[106] What traits are the opposite of meekness? Why would the meek be those most worthy and prepared to inherit the earth?

EVE

Blessed are they which do hunger and thirst after righteousness:
for they shall be filled.

1. When faced with whether to multiply and replenish the earth or avoid the fruit of the knowledge of good and evil (and stay in the Garden), Eve eventually used her agency to advance mankind while seemingly disobeying another law. Although much of religious tradition thinks this was wrong—a sin—modern revelation teaches, as Elder Boyd K. Packer explains, "the Fall came by transgression of a law, but there was no sin connected with it."[107] What does this quote mean? Are there different levels or categories of laws that apply differently per context or that supersede other laws? Consider temporal laws vs. eternal laws, higher laws vs. lower laws, and the letter of the law vs. the spirit of the law.

2. The word *transgression* comes from the Latin *trans,* meaning "to move from one state to another" or "beyond" or "across," and *gress* means "to go."[108] Aside from simply moving from a state of innocence and bliss into the mortal world with all its weeds and storms, what other states of being and knowledge did Eve move beyond or to? What wisdom and blessings might she have gained that only come from experience? What experiences do you feel moved you "beyond" into a new state of understanding or wisdom or being?

3. Imagine being the first woman to navigate mortality! What emotions and thoughts do you think Eve may have experienced? What "firsts" might she have been awed by? What "tools" and spiritual gifts might she have used to find her way through the emotional jungle before her? Which of them may also apply to your "firsts" here in mortality?

4. The Bible promises that those who hunger and thirst after righteousness will be filled. This verse of scripture is clarified and expanded upon in the Book of Mormon.[109] What is it we will be filled with? Why is the distinction important? What does it mean to you to "be filled"?

5. Women of Christ, who hunger and thirst after righteousness, will need to learn to recognize the adversary's tactics and speak up amongst their sisters when modern (or ancient and repurposed) ideas are harmful or when injustice and cruelty must be stopped. But how do we approach this process and calling with integrity and Christlike love? What questions do we ask ourselves and what processes do we pursue in determining when and how to speak and act in the name of truth?

ESTHER

Blessed are the merciful: for they shall obtain mercy.

1. When Esther had to make a decision that not only affected her, but the lives of her people, she needed to put her own concerns aside and discover the Lord's will. Have you ever been in a situation where you didn't know the best direction to take, so you had to seek out the Lord's will? How did you go about making that decision and hearing His answer?

2. Esther needed mercy from her husband, the king, who had approved an edict to destroy her people. How desperate she must have felt. Yet she bravely made her request. Like the Savior in Gethsemane praying for mercy upon all our souls, Esther found herself turning to her Maker as well and pleading for mercy for her people. Knowing that the Savior will extend His mercy to us, how does that influence how we extend mercy to those in our lives?

3. When Esther put her own well-being on the line to seek mercy from the king, she prepared for the event through fasting and prayer. What are ways that you can prepare to seek the Lord's help in times of great need?

4. After fasting and praying for three days, the time arrived for Esther to petition the king for mercy on her people. In the end, Esther's fears did not come to pass, yet the process of putting her faith in the Lord strengthened her and her people. Have you experienced a time when you've overcome a trial and looked back to see the Lord's hand in helping you?

5. President Dieter F. Uchtdorf counseled us to lay our burdens at the Savior's feet. In Esther's story, we see an example of this as she prepares to plead for her people's lives. How can we lay our own burdens at the Lord's feet? What are the steps we must take?

HANNAH

Blessed are the poor in spirit: for theirs is the kingdom of heaven.

1. We may not always understand the Lord's will. In Hannah's case, she was barren for many years, then was blessed with the miracle of becoming pregnant. Her prayers were answered eventually, but in the Lord's time. How can we find strength and comfort when the Lord's timetable is different than what we're hoping for?

2. Whether a trial is short-term or lifelong, at times we experience feeling poor in spirit. Our humility increases, and we come to understand how dependent we are on God. This in turn brings us closer to the Lord. Knowing this, what are some ways we can acknowledge and find gratitude in our trials?

3. The Lord has promised to grant the poor in spirit the kingdom of heaven. How does this knowledge bring us comfort when we are living through difficult challenges?
4. Like Hannah, who recognized she needed God's help, we, too, can seek counsel and blessings through fasting and humble prayer. What are some other ways you've received answers to prayers or found needed counsel?
5. We are all from different walks of life and have experienced various types of trials. We might consider poor-in-spirit experiences as opportunities to draw closer to the Lord, since we are asked to rely on Him in all things. What methods do you use to draw closer to the Lord?

MARY

Blessed are the pure in heart: for they shall see God.

1. Mary was told by an angel that she was to be the mother of the Messiah. What a mission to be presented with. No doubt this was a heavy moment for Mary despite the awe and spiritual strength she may have felt as the Lord buoyed her up. Imagine what thoughts or feelings you would have. How does this compare to your own experiences with meaningful but difficult callings and circumstances in your own life? Ponder these roles, callings, challenges, and gifts in your life. These can be heavy burdens but also blessings. How can you find the strength and direction to magnify each while also finding peace and balance?
2. When we are pure in heart, the Lord can better use us to be His hands to fulfil the many missions we each have been given, whether they last a few months or a lifetime and whether they are a joy to fulfil or sometimes deeply difficult to manage. What experiences have you (or friends or family) had that purified your heart regarding a difficult challenge—changing your view of it?
3. What does it mean to be pure in heart? What does it look like? What does it feel like? How is it connected to the process of sanctification?

4. How did Mary cope with the intense emotions that must have filled her heart, knowing the breadth and depth of her mission and that of her son's? His mission caused her great joy and great sorrow. One telling reveal is that with her experiences, Mary "kept all these things, and pondered them."[110] What was she pondering? How might pondering your experiences help you to bear them, shape them, appreciate them, and see them in a new light?

5. It's difficult to comprehend the special way Mary saw God—how she may have understood the mission of the Savior and how hers intertwined with it. And she literally saw the workings of God and angels on the earth. However, we know from scripture that it is not always the external seeing of divine power that gives us new—pure—hearts. There are many ways to see God, even now in mortality. Among them, as our hearts become more like His, are the gifts of seeing God's hand in our lives and seeing as God sees. When have you seen God's hand in your life? Have you had an experience when you felt you were able to see as God sees?

ABISH

Blessed are the peacemakers: for they shall be called the children of God.

1. Abish was not able to share her testimony or knowledge of God with her people during most of her life. Some of us may find ourselves in this type of situation as well. How can we remain faithful and nurture our testimonies when we aren't able to openly worship in the gospel?

2. Abish was prepared to share her testimony when the time came. How can we stay prepared for a time that we might be called upon to share our testimonies, serve, or influence others?

3. Abish originally became converted to the gospel after she was taught by her father. But to maintain her conversion, she had to grow her own faith and develop her own relationship with the Lord. What are the key things in your life that have helped you maintain your own testimony independent of anyone else's faith journey?

4. When at last Abish could share her true beliefs, there was still a risk of her own people turning against her or condemning her for taking the side of a Nephite. Regardless, Abish pushed past her fears and apprehensions, then followed the promptings of the Spirit and became an important voice. Have there been times when you've shared your testimony even though it was difficult to do?

5. When Abish shared her testimony and quelled the rising panic of her people, she acted as a peacemaker. Being a peacemaker isn't always easy, but what are some situations in which you've acted as a peacemaker and then later saw the Spirit's prompting?

SARIAH

Blessed are they which are persecuted for righteousness' sake:
for theirs is the kingdom of heaven.

1. History holds a sacred and terrible record of those who have endured persecution for the sake of Christ and the gospel. Can you think of saints from any period who have endured public reviling, shaming, or the maligning of their character and intentions of their hearts? What did those individuals do to cope with and overcome such challenges? What decisions did they make, and what perspectives did they have?

2. Consider, alternatively, the painful and poignantly personal experience of prolonged rejection, mockery, or angry chastisement from those who should be most understanding of why we stand for righteousness—our parents, children, spouses, siblings, friends, and others we may deeply love. Have you or others you love found yourself facing such circumstances? What have you done to seek peace and unification? How do you balance a righteous example with love for those who can't understand your beliefs? How can you support individuals who are bearing such burdens?

3. Sariah likely experienced many of the persecutions listed above. There may have been days when she felt she had to choose between God and

her family—or between family members. What are possible ways Sariah may have navigated such difficulty? Did she ever struggle in her faith? Did she have resolutions to such struggle? What gifts of the spirit might she have drawn upon during her many trials?

4. The trial of Sariah's faith may have given her opportunities to find meaning in her suffering and greater purpose. What new perspectives have you gained from circumstances in which you learned to bravely put the gospel and Christ first? What qualities have you developed or improved upon? What examples have you gleaned wisdom from?

5. President Joseph F. Smith once spoke on what it means to rest in Christ—a critical focus we must develop when facing the winds of persecution and adversity in the cause of Christ:

> "It means that through the love of God I have been won over to Him . . . no power can turn me aside from the straight and narrow path that leads back into the presence of God."[111]

> Brigham Young previously shared this thought:

> "Suppose that you could see yourselves . . . after you have . . . obtained eternal salvation. . . . [t]hen look back upon your lives here, and see the losses [and] crosses . . . ; you would be constrained to exclaim, 'but what of all that? Those things were but for a moment, and we are now here.'"[112]

How do these thoughts on the eternal perspective affect your thinking about this life's difficulties? Do you think the "great reward in heaven" the beatitude promises is tied to an eternal perspective?[113] Does developing an eternal perspective in this life mean that we will cease feeling grief, anger, or fear, or never struggle? If not, consider the prophets' quotes above. What might having an eternal perspective mean, and what might it shift in your life?

ENDNOTES

1. See Matthew 4:23.
2. See Matthew 4:24–25; the multitudes came from Galilee, Decapolis, Jerusalem, Judea, and outside Jordan.
3. See 3 Nephi 12.
4. See *Hymns*, no. 131.
5. The Sermon on the Mount took place around Pentecost, traditionally fifty days after Passover week. The gathering of these multitudes was at a location that would soon become known as the Mount of Beatitudes, a holy place where Christ delivered His Sermon on the Mount. This was a hill in "the area north of Capernaum because that is where 'the mountain' near the town rises up. To the south, of course, lies the Sea of Galilee" (S. Kent Brown, *New Testament Commentary: The Testimony of Luke* [Provo, UT: Brigham Young University, 2015], 349).
6. "Joy and Spiritual Survival," *Ensign* or *Liahona*, October 2016, https://www.churchofjesuschrist.org/study/general-conference/2016/10/joy-and-spiritual-survival?lang=eng.
7. D&C 50:41.
8. D&C 122:7.
9. D&C 88:6.
10. Alma 7:11.
11. D&C 88:41.
12. Hebrews 12:2.
13. *Hymns*, no. 131 (capitalization adjusted for ease in reading).
14. See Genesis 11:29.
15. See Genesis 11:30.
16. See Genesis 12:2.
17. See Genesis 12:7.
18. D&C 132:65.
19. Genesis 16:2.
20. Genesis 17:17.
21. Genesis 21:9.

22 James E. Talmage, *Jesus the Christ*, https://www.churchofjesuschrist.org/study/manual/jesus-the-christ/chapter-17?lang=eng.

23 Isaiah 40:28–31.

24 Ruth 1:8–9.

25 Ruth 1:14–17.

26 Ruth 1:20–21.

27 Ruth 2:2.

28 See Leviticus 19:9–10.

29 David A. Bednar, "Meek and Lowly of Heart," *Ensign* or *Liahona*, May 2018, https://www.churchofjesuschrist.org/study/general-conference/2018/04/meek-and-lowly-of-heart?lang=eng.

30 Mosiah 24:15; emphasis added.

31 Ruth 2:10–12.

32 Ruth 3:1.

33 Lying at Boaz's feet on a certain night; see Ruth 3:4.

34 Wayne E. Brickey, *Making Sense of Suffering* (Salt Lake City: Deseret Book, 2001), 51.

35 Genesis 3:1.

36 Genesis 3:4–5.

37 Conversation with Dr. Nehama Aschkenasy, in Beverly Campbell, *Eve and the Choice Made in Eden*, 1st edition (Salt Lake City: Deseret Book, 2009), 71.

38 Nehama Aschkenasy, *Eve's Journey* (1986), 42, quoted in Beverly Campbell, *Eve and the Choice Made in Eden*.

39 See Genesis 2–3.

40 Boyd K. Packer, *Things of the Soul* (Salt Lake City: Bookcraft, 1996), 49.

41 Moses 4:12.

42 Richard D. Draper, S. Kent Brown, and Michael D. Rhodes, *The Pearl of Great Price: A Verse-by-Verse Commentary* (Salt Lake City: Deseret Book, 2005), 43.

43 Moses 4:13.

44 Collins Dictionary, s.v. "trans-," accessed August 2021, https://www.collinsdictionary.com/dictionary/english/trans; and Online Etymology Dictionary, s.v. "trans-," accessed August 2021, https://www.etymonline.com/word/transgression.

45 See Moses 6:12.

46 3 Nephi 12:6; emphasis added.

47 See also Beverly Campbell's interesting discussion on women in the last days, *Eve and the Choice Made in Eden* [2002], 78.

48 Moses 5:11.

49 James E. Talmage, *Jesus the Christ*, https://www.churchofjesuschrist.org/study/manual/jesus-the-christ/chapter-17?lang=eng.

50 Matthew 5:7.

51 Moroni 7:45.

52 See Esther 1:17–20.

53 Truman G. Madsen, "How and Why Would God Give Men Weaknesses?" *Ensign*, February 1985, https://www.churchofjesuschrist.org/study/ensign/1985/02/i-have-a-question/how-and-why-would-god-give-men-weaknesses?lang=eng.

54 Esther 4:15–16.

55 Esther 5:2–4.

56 D&C 88:40.

57 Dieter F. Uchtdorf, "The Merciful Obtain Mercy," *Ensign* or *Liahona*, April 2012, https://www.churchofjesuschrist.org/study/liahona/2012/05/sunday-morning-session/the-merciful-obtain-mercy?lang=eng.

58 Luke 6:20.

59 *Book of Mormon Student Manual, Religion 121–122* (2009), chapter 41, https://www.churchofjesuschrist.org/study/manual/book-of-mormon-student-manual/chapter-41-3-nephi-12-14?lang=eng.

60 1 Samuel 1:6.

61 1 Samuel 1:8.

62 1 Samuel 1:15.

63 1 Samuel 1:17.

64 1 Samuel 1:11.

65 3 Nephi 12:3.

66 Truman Madsen, "Joseph Smith's Vision of the Global Church," BYU-Idaho Devotional, *Religious Lecture Series*, January 29, 2005, https://www.byui.edu/devotionals/brother-truman-g-madsen.

67 Abraham 3:26.

68 D&C 64:32.

69 Luke 1:26–31.

70 Luke 1:38.

71 Luke 1:46–49.

72 Luke 2:34–35.

73 Luke 2:19.

74 Truman G. Madsen, "How Can I Become Closer to the Lord?" *Meridian Magazine*, January 19, 2001, https://latterdaysaintmag.com/article-1-906/.

75　1 Corinthians 13:12.

76　See D&C 121:45.

77　See 1 Corinthians 13.

78　1 Corinthians 2:16.

79　Luke 1:38.

80　Job 42:5.

81　Luke 1:46–47.

82　Hebrews 12:2.

83　Matthew 5:9.

84　1 Nephi 11:35.

85　Alma 19:16.

86　See Alma 18:18.

87　See Alma 18:35.

88　See Alma 18:42.

89　See Alma 19:8, 12.

90　See Alma 19:13.

91　See Alma 19:17–18.

92　Alma 19:28.

93　Alma 19:28.

94　See Alma 19:29.

95　Russell M. Nelson, "Blessed Are the Peacemakers," *Ensign* or *Liahona*, October 2002, https://www.churchofjesuschrist.org/study/general-conference/2002/10/blessed-are-the-peacemakers?lang=eng.

96　D&C 98:16.

97　Psalm 118:16.

98　See 1 Nephi 1–2.

99　1 Nephi 5:8.

100　Henry B. Eyring, "Holiness and the Plan of Happiness," *Ensign* or *Liahona*, October 2019, https://www.churchofjesuschrist.org/study/general-conference/2019/10/51eyring?lang=eng.

101　Ulisses Soares, "Take Up Our Cross," *Ensign* or *Liahona*, November 2019, https://www.churchofjesuschrist.org/study/ensign/2019/11/55soares?lang=eng.

102　*Teachings of the Presidents of the Church: Joseph F. Smith* (2011), https://www.churchofjesuschrist.org/study/manual/teachings-joseph-f-smith/chapter-48?lang=eng.

103　1 Nephi 5:8.

104 Brigham Young, in *Deseret News*, November 9, 1859, 1.

105 David A. Bednar, "Meek and Lowly of Heart," churchofjesuschrist.org, May 2018, https://www.churchofjesuschrist.org/study/general-conference/2018/04/meek-and-lowly-of-heart?lang=eng.

106 Wayne E. Brickey, *Making Sense of Suffering* (2001), 51–52.

107 Boyd K. Packer, *Things of the Soul* (1996), 49.

108 See *Collins Dictionary*, https://www.collinsdictionary.com/dictionary/english/trans; see also Online Etymology Dictionary, https://www.etymonline.com/word/transgression.

109 See 3 Nephi 12:6.

110 Luke 2:19.

111 "Finding Rest in Christ," *Teachings of the Presidents of the Church: Joseph F. Smith* (2011), churchofjesuschrist.org, https://www.churchofjesuschrist.org/study/manual/teachings-joseph-f-smith/chapter-48?lang=eng.

112 Brigham Young, in *Deseret News*, November 9, 1859, 1.

113 Matthew 5:12.

Pull Quotes in Order

1. Russell M. Nelson, "Women—of Infinite Worth," *Ensign*, November 1989.
2. Jeffrey R. Holland, "Behold Thy Mother," *Ensign* or *Liahona*, November 2015.
3. Thomas S. Monson, "Models to Follow," *Ensign* or *Liahona*, November 2002.
4. Thomas S. Monson, "Models to Follow," *Ensign* or *Liahona*, November 2002.
5. Russell M. Nelson, "A Plea to My Sisters," *Ensign* or *Liahona*, November 2015.
6. Jeffrey R. Holland, "The Ministry of Angels," *Ensign* or *Liahona*, November 2008.
7. Thomas S. Monson, "May You Have Courage," *Ensign* or *Liahona*, May 2009.
8. Thomas S. Monson, "May You Have Courage," *Ensign* or *Liahona*, May 2009.
9. Cecil O. Samuelson Jr., "Our Duty to God," *Ensign*, November 2001.
10. Julie B. Beck, "Mothers Who Know," *Ensign* or *Liahona*, November 2007.
11. L. Whitney Clayton, "Whatsoever He Saith Unto You, Do It," *Ensign* or *Liahona*, May 2017.
12. Russell M. Nelson, "Women—of Infinite Worth," *Ensign*, November 1989.
13. Neil L. Andersen, "Spiritually Defining Memories," *Ensign* or *Liahona*, May 2020.
14. Elaine S. Dalton, " Love Her Mother," *Ensign* or *Liahona*, November 2012.
15. Elaine L. Jack, "Look Up and Press On," *Ensign*, May 1992.
16. Elaine L. Jack, "Look Up and Press On," *Ensign*, May 1992.

ART CREDITS

Cover: *Guiding Light* © Annie Henrie Nader, www.anniehenrie.com. Image adjusted with the artist's permission

Page iv: *Garden Meditation* © Annie Henrie Nader, www.anniehenrie.com

Page 6: *Sarah Laughed and Rejoiced* © Julie Rogers, julierogersart.com

Page 12: *Gleaning Blessings* © Beki Tobiasson, bekitobiassonartist.com

Page 18: *Eve* © Mandy Jane Williams, www.mandyjanewilliamsart.com

Page 26: *The Faith of Queen Esther* © Sandra Bangerter Rast, sandrarast.com

Page 32: *Hannah's Offering* © Elizabeth Jean Stanley, Elizabethstanleyart.com

Page 38: *Little Mother* © Annie Henrie Nader, www.anniehenrie.com

Page 44: *Ready to Receive* © Annie Henrie Nader, www.anniehenrie.com

Page 50: *Light Vessel* © Annie Henrie Nader, www.anniehenrie.com

Page 58: *The Shepherd* © Annie Henrie Nader, www.anniehenrie.com